MAMA
WHY IS MY FLOWER
WILTING?

Written by:
Nakayla C. Leggett

Illustrated by:
Hatice Bayramoglu

ISBN-13: 978-1727847277
ISBN-10: 172784727X

DEDICATION

This book is dedicated to my wonderful children Kassidy and Malcolm. I hope that you continue to blossom and encourage those connected to you to blossom as well.

"It's morning time mommy," Kassidy said as her eyes lit up. She was excited for her first day of 4th grade.

Kassidy lived in a small town in North Carolina named Elizabethtown with her mom, dad and big brother, Malcolm.

She went through her morning checklist faster than lightning! Washed face, check, brushed teeth, check, fixed bed, check.

BEEP! BEEP! "KASSIDY, YOUR BUS IS HERE," her mom yelled. So she kissed her flower goodbye and out the door she went, skipping the whole way!

Kassidy had a great day at school and was eager to tell her mom about all the new friends she made!

Everything was going great until Chloe transferred to Kassidy's class the 3rd month of school.

Kassidy didn't come home with the same burst of glee as before. She seemed to not want to talk about her day anymore. Whereas she once barely made it in the house before yelling to her mother about all the fun she had.

Kassidy started to say mean things to her brother, not listen to her parents and spent most of her time in her room away from the family.

Things began to get so bad that Kassidy started to throw tantrums in the mornings before school so her mom wouldn't make her go, but it didn't work.

She even stopped watering and caring for the beautiful flower she once adored and cherished.

Kassidy's mom felt sad because she didn't know what was wrong with her baby girl.

One day her mom sent the boys out for the day and decided to have a mommy, daughter day.

Kassidy and her mom baked cookies, painted nails and watched movies.

In the middle of all the fun, mom asked Kassidy why she didn't enjoy school anymore.

At first, Kassidy got really quiet and held her head low. Her mom asked again and this time Kassidy told her mom that a new girl, Chloe, was calling her names and saying mean things about her hair and clothes.

Kassidy had started to play and eat alone at school to avoid crying from Chloe's mean words.

Mom patted Kassidy on the back and gave her a hug. Mom looked over at Kassidy's once beautifully bloomed flower and saw it was half wilted. Mom told her to go get a glass of water and water the flower. Kassidy did as she was told.

As Kassidy watered the flower she asked, "Mama why is my flower wilting?" Her mom responded, "Flowers need to feel loved and cared for, just like us."

"What did you do every day for your flower Kassidy", mom asked. Kassidy explained that every morning and night she would talk to her flower, open the blinds for sunshine and water it once a week. She quickly said, "oh no, I haven't done that in a few weeks."

"Why wouldn't you feed your plant apple juice and chips," mom asked. "Mama that's crazy, that would kill my flower", Kassidy was giggling so hard she couldn't control it.

"Exactly baby girl, you feed your flower things that will help it continue to grow strong and remain beautiful. You see our brains are the same way with our thoughts and feelings. Sometimes we allow the negative things people say about us to become our feeding sources."

"Those things start to make us wilt over time. We start to feel uncomfortable feelings such as sadness and anger. Sometimes we try to make other people feel just as bad as we are feeling."

"But I don't want to feel that way mama", Kassidy cried. Mom explained to Kassidy that she must learn to feed herself things that make her feel good.

"Every morning before I leave for work I tell myself I am going to have a great day, I even tell myself my hair is pretty and maybe twirl in the mirror", Mom said smiling.

"You are in control of your brain, so only allow thoughts in that will help you. Throw out those that make your flower wilt. Also, remember to talk to someone when throwing the negative thoughts out becomes too difficult because it gets hard sometimes for everyone."

Kassidy woke up the next morning for school in a better mood, looked in the mirror as she styled her curly afro with a blue headband and decided she would ignore Chloe's negative words.

That afternoon when she returned home she was excited to tell her mom that her day was not perfect, but better. She tried to ignore Chloe by replacing the negative thoughts with positive ones. She admitted that it was hard and helped a little. She was hopeful it will get better over time.

Kassidy continued to feed herself positive thoughts and she continued to gain strength to ignore other people's mean words. And look her flower is blooming beautifully!